my
MUSLIM
FAITH

About this book

The titles in the *My Faith* collection are designed to introduce young children to the six world faiths and each focuses on a child and his or her family from a particular faith community. Whilst the approach and the language level are appropriate for young readers, some of the key concepts will need to be supported by sensitive clarification by an adult. The Notes for Teachers and Parents on pages 4 and 5 provide extra information to help develop children's knowledge and understanding of the different beliefs and traditions.

First published in this edition in 2006 by
Evans Brothers Limited
2A Portman Mansions
Chiltern St
London W1U 6NR

Printed in China by WKT Company Limited

British Library Cataloguing in Publication Data

Knight, Khadijah
  My Muslim faith. - (My Faith)
  1. Islam - Juvenile literature 2. Muslim children - Religious life - Juvenile literature
  3. Muslims - Juvenile literature
  I. Title
  297
  ISBN 023753229 8
  13 digit ISBN (from 1 January 2007) 9780237 53229 1

Editor: Su Swallow
Design: D.R. ink
Production: Jenny Mulvanny
Reading consultant: Lesley Clark, Reading and Language Information Centre
Series consultant: Alison Seaman, The National Society's Religious Education Centre
Photography: Muhsin Kilby

Acknowledgements

The author and publishers would like to thank Tayeba Sharif and her family, Muhammad, Maryam, Zayneb, Safia and also the Islamic Consultancy and Education Services, for their help in making this book.

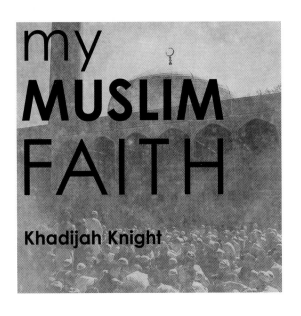

my MUSLIM FAITH

Khadijah Knight

Evans

Contents

Notes for Teachers and Parents

Pages 6/7 Islam is the faith and way of life of over a billion people. Muslims come from every racial background. A person may choose to become Muslim at any stage of their life by reciting the Shahadah: 'I bear witness that there is no god except Allah and that Muhammad is the Messenger of Allah'. Although Muslims wear various styles of clothing and have different ethnic customs, they are united by the beliefs and practices of Islam. The word Islam means peace and a Muslim finds peace through obedience to Allah.

Pages 8/9 Allah is the Arabic and Islamic name for the One True God. Muslims believe that Allah alone created the universe out of nothing. The Oneness of Allah is called Tawhid and belief in it is central to Islam. Allah is the designer, sustainer and provider and has ultimate control of the outcome of events. Allah's power is so great that many 'beautiful names' are used to describe His attributes. Muslims never try to draw or otherwise visually depict Allah.

Pages 10/11 To recite salah and communicate with Allah, Muslims must be clean. They say the intention to make wudu and begin washing hands, mouth, nose, face, forearms, feet and ankles three times in running water, and wipe head, ears and neck. Wudu is refreshing and marks a transition from worldly activity to a spiritual state. During salah men and women must be modestly dressed. Men wear hats and women use big scarves to cover their hair, neck and chest. Some women keep a special cover called a chador to wear only for prayer.

Pages 12/13 Muslims can pray in any clean place, at home, school, work, mosque or in the open air. The set times of prayer are calculated by the position of the sun, so vary from day to day throughout the year. Fajr is prayed between the first light of dawn and sunrise, Zuhr just after midday, Asr at mid afternoon, Maghrib at sunset and Isha about an hour and a half after sunset. The positions of salah - standing, bowing, kneeling and prostrating - demonstrate uprightness, respect, gratitude and readiness to do what Allah wants.

Pages 14/15 The Ka'bah, a cube-shaped structure, is the first house made for the worship of the One True God. It was built, over 4,000 years ago, by the Prophet Ibrahim 🕮 and his son Ismail 🕮. In time their message was forgotten and false gods and idols were placed inside. When Allah's message was revealed to the Prophet Muhammad 🕮, he convinced people that idol worship was wrong. He destroyed the idols and restored the Ka'bah to a place of monotheistic belief. Wherever they are in the world Muslims turn in the direction of the Ka'bah to pray.

Pages 16/17 Muslims believe that the Qur'an was revealed to the Prophet Muhammad 🕮 by the Angel Jibril over a period of 23 years. He learned Allah's divine words by heart and taught them to his followers. They were written down in the order that the Angel instructed. The Arabic words of the Qur'an are unchanged since their revelation [610-633 CE]. No matter where they live or what language they speak, Muslims always recite the Qur'anic words of salah in Arabic. Millions of Muslims world-wide know the entire Qur'an by heart. The Qur'an is always handled with great care and respect by Muslims.

Pages 18/19 Muslims trace the origins of Islam to the first man and the first Prophet Adam ﷺ. They believe that Allah sent His messengers to guide every nation and tribe, to teach people how to worship Him and behave towards His creation. The Prophet Muhammad ﷺ is Allah's final messenger. He is the living example of how to behave as Allah instructed in the Qur'an. Whenever Muslims mention his name they also say, ' the peace and blessings of Allah upon him and his family.' In print, this is shown as an Arabic colophon, as on these pages.

Pages 20/21 There is no one design for mosque buildings, nor do mosques have to have either a dome or a minaret. Depending on where they are in the world mosques will be built in the style of that country and in the materials available. In Britain there are more than 2,000 mosques to serve the community. Some are purpose built, others are converted from factories, churches and synagogues. All mosques have a prayer hall where no shoes are worn and a simple Mihrab on one wall showing the direction of the Ka'bah.

Pages 22/23 The Islamic lunar calendar began when the Prophet Muhammad ﷺ moved from Makkah to Madinah to establish the first Islamic community. Each of the twelve months begins with the sighting of the new moon and lasts for 29 or 30 days till the next moon. The Islamic year is about eleven days shorter than the 365 day solar year. Each year the Islamic months start 11 days earlier than the previous year, so none of the Muslim festivals are fixed to a particular season.

Pages 24/25 The Hajj is pilgrimage to Makkah and the holy places in the surrounding area. All Muslims must try to undertake this journey at least once in their lives, if they can afford it and have good health. The Hajj takes place during the 8th-12th of Dhul Hijjah - the twelfth month of the Islamic year. During Hajj pilgrims commemorate and re-enact events in the lives of the Prophets Ibrahim, Ismail and Muhammad - peace and blessings on them all.

Pages 26/27 Muslims throughout the world celebrate two main religious festivals. These are called Id, which literally means recurring happiness. The first, Id ul Fitr, occurs at the start of the month following Ramadan and celebrates the completion of the fast. The second, which takes place at the time of Hajj-pilgrimage, is called Id ul Adha - the feast of sacrifice. It commemorates the Prophet Ibrahim's willing obedience to Allah. Early in the morning on both Ids, Muslims gather at the largest mosque or open prayer ground to listen to the Id talk and recite the Id salah.

Pages 28/29 There are over 400,000 young Muslims at school in Britain. The majority attend county schools. Many also have Qur'an lessons at their local mosque school - madrassa - several evenings each week. As well as learning to pray and recite the Qur'an in Arabic, many Muslim children are bilingual. Muslim families know that it is their responsibility to teach their children, directly and by good example, the Islamic values of honesty, respect and modesty. Children and their families appreciate when schools provide opportunities for all pupils to learn from and about Islam.

My name
is Tayeba.
I am a Muslim.

We believe that **Allah** alone made the world. He made the plants and the animals.

Allah made the sun and the sky.
He made the moon and the stars.
He gave us everything we need to live.

What does Allah teach you?

Allah teaches us to look after what He made and to live in peace.

I like looking after plants. I give them water to grow.

Water is good for many things.
Muslims wash before praying.

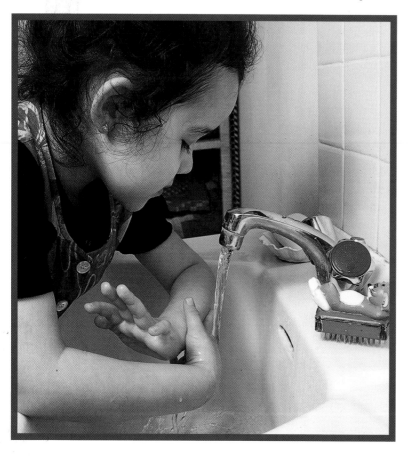

This washing is called wudu.
The prayers are called salah.

Why are you putting on special clothes?

When we pray, boys put on hats and girls wear scarves.

This shows that we respect Allah.

We have five special times
for salah every day.

The first time is before sunrise.
The last time is after dark.

Where do you pray?

We can pray in any clean place.
We use mats like this one to make sure
there is no dirt where we say our salah.

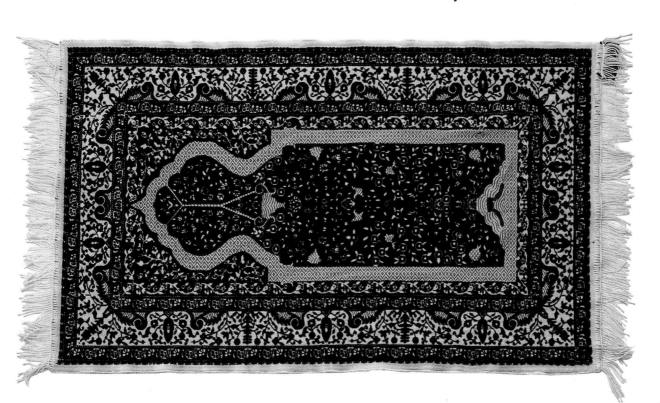

We always place the mat facing in the direction of the **Ka'bah**, in Makkah.

The Ka'bah is a special place for Muslims.

What do you say in your prayers?

We thank Allah for all the good things he gives us.

The words are in Arabic. Some of the words are in our holy book called the **Qur'an.**

How do you learn the Arabic words?

My big brother Muhammad teaches me to read the Qur'an.

I practise every day.

This Arabic writing says Allah.

Our uncle tells us stories about Allah,
and about Allah's messenger,
the Prophet Muhammad ﷺ.

The Prophet Muhammadﷺ told people to be kind to each other and share what we have.

My sister and I give some of our pocket money to the mosque.

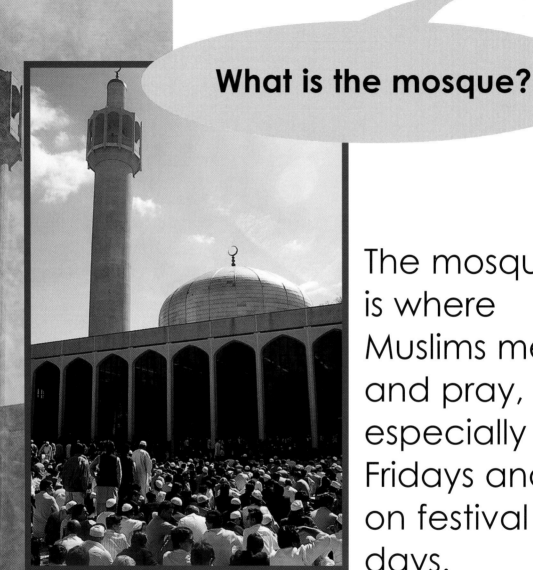

What is the mosque?

The mosque is where Muslims meet and pray, especially on Fridays and on festival days.

Inside the mosque is a place
that shows the direction
of the Ka'bah.

I like the holy month of **Ramadan.**
It starts when we see the new moon.
This moon calendar shows us when
Ramadan is.

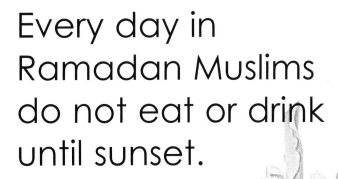

Every day in Ramadan Muslims do not eat or drink until sunset.

We break our fast with dates and a drink.

What other special times do Muslims have?

Every year in the Hajj month, Muslims from all over the world travel to Makkah.

The men and boys wear special white clothes.

When our family gets together,
my dad often tells us about
his journey to Makkah.

Some Muslim festivals are called **Id** days. On Id days we go to the mosque to pray.
Then we have fun in the park with our friends.

We send Id cards to our friends.
The cards wish them blessings
and happiness.

We don't go to school on Id days, but our school has a celebration after Id so all the children can share our fun.

This is my mum and my
new baby sister Maryam.

As she gets bigger I am going
to teach her all about Allah
and being a Muslim.

Glossary

 These are the Arabic words for 'the peace and blessings of Allah be upon him', which Muslims say after the name of the Prophet Muhammad ﷺ.

Allah - The Arabic name for God.

Id - Happy festival. There are two every year, one at the end of Ramadan, one at Hajj time.

Ka'bah - The first house built for people to pray to the One God.

Qur'an - The book which has all the special messages Allah gave for Muhammad ﷺ to teach people.

Ramadan - The 9th month of the Muslim year. Muslims do not eat or drink anything during daylight.

Index